Habere Cervisiam

Poems by CL Bledsoe

These poems appeared in similar forms in the following journals:

As It Ought To Be, Bourgeon, Emerge Literary Journal, Eunoia Review, Fixator Press, Flight of the Dragonfly Journal, Impspired, Lothlorien Poetry Journal, Medusa's Kitchen, One Art Poetry Journal, Phantom Kangaroo, Right Hand Pointing, Setu, SoFloPoJo, The Sparrow's Trombone, Spillwords, Stripes Magazine, Suisun Valley Review, Synchronized Chaos, Stirring, Taj Mahal Review, Tell-Tale Inklings, Ten Million Flies, Tiger Shark, Trouvaille Review, Unlikely Stories, Words and Whispers.

"My Teen Years in Mothballs" appeared in *The Alien Buddha Goes Pop* anthology.

Contents

Fairly Young Heave-Hos and Shrifts of Indeterminate Length

The idea that life would just give
away lemons. That God would think
to close a door or open a window
rather than let the bugs in and the heat out.

If only damns and wide berths.
If only a doubt or any benefits.

No one wants a used arm or either side
of a hand, no matter how well you know
them. Maybe to hold, to be held. But at what
cost? They may loan an ax, but they expect
the ropes back. The same is true of boots,
and tickets out of here are nontransferable.

If you want a rest, or a chance, you have
to take it. The bank owns every inch,
and they give away nothing. And what
you give, it never comes back.

Bring Out Your Dead

A woman goes from bed to bed,
each night, pulling her cart. "Bring
out your dead," she says. Workers wake,
shuffle to the window, where
she's squared up to receive
what they dump. One drops the last time
he skinny dipped with his cousin,
before they learned shame. That
cousin is dead now, or a corporate
lawyer. Another, his hands, stained
with charcoal and paper cuts, paint
under the nails, palms smudged. Leaving
them clean and soft. At each house,
the bodies pile up, eyes brighter
than those who collapse back
into bed. Tomorrow is a big
day. The Kowalski Report. Traffic.

A Moon Bear Named Carl

I went outside to catch the moon
bear as it fell. My first mistake.
Imagine fur so thick wind sheer
gave up and went over to its friend
Dave's house to complain. The softest
murder, the warmest throat rend.

I was trying to be of use. I watched

it slip, through my homemade
telescope. Stumbling home from
the bar. Too much pickled salmon
and mead. It tripped, fell clean
across a crater, bounced off a distracted
seal in the Sea of Tranquility,

and ricocheted toward DC. Bright

honey trail oozing across the sky.
Arms out, elbows braced, I aimed
my hope for its squirming belly
to keep the greedy ground wanting.
I needed a fourth for bridge. Now,
I only need a second and third.

Consider the Mountain's Feelings

Even the best outlined plans shrink
when laid out to dry. Inevitability is
a raw deal unless you've bought
stock in the undertaker. The arrogance
of the radiator. The air's thirsty voice.
Just because that time is never coming
back doesn't mean I can't write it a letter.
I put your little eyes to my ear so I can hear
that place you're still allowed in. I wish
you could stay there forever, but it would
be nice if you got the jokes in movies I like.
Here is a list of problems I can't quantify:
why is it that our most beautiful parts are
those we've cast off? Is anything ever
worth making if it will only disappoint?
It's a question of perspective, which is
another way of saying accepting failure
as somebody else's responsibility. Is
the problem of feeling comfortable
in the world really just one of accessories?
Do you think about me or just what
I've done for you? Guest rooms are
for cowards. The arrogance of unused real
estate. Let's not make a big scene
about how we've failed each other in front
of the children. I'll try to do better, every day.
That's what I have to teach you: it's not
in the journey, the choice of footwear,
or even the quality of compliments paid

the weather. It's in how well you nod
and smile along with the mountain's
complaints, and whether you think of them
again, once you're home, warm, and safe.
Did you come just to have a thing to climb?
And once there, how will you get down?

Dumpster Horse

Morning falls hard, still drunk but
having a good time. Everyone can
hear it put its finger to its mouth
and ask the carpet to ignore the smell.
Beer holders nest in the corner, raising
little families; cars jabber in the trees,
looking for anyone to get inside them.
Someone should write a letter
to someone who still knows how
to read. Morning tastes the way
your goodbye hit my good intentions,
which is to say unable to take a fucking
joke, which is to say, life. Like you're
the only one who's dying today. Get
over yourself. I'll loan you a ladder
if you need one and directions on
which way is up. I suspect some
of us are hiding in the basement, waiting
for the storm to pass. (Hint: try opening
the curtains.) You didn't realize, you
and I were each other's suns. Sometimes
you fall in love with the rain just so you
can feel chilly in the wind. The beige
face of regret has a carefully curated list
of questions, when you have a moment.
First, forget everything I said but mostly
what I did and feel sorry for me. The stop-
hitting-yourself school of relationship
counseling. Fuck me if I can't take a joke.

Drag Your Tape Gun Across the Night

Boxes seem to dent the floor   their placement,
          a weight that sucks the future in.

So long, I've waited to wait for the wait,
          which will begin any minute now.

These things I've dragged across hell's creation;
          detritus abandoned   Here's a woman's hand
          that forgot me   and a face I've forgotten
Scowling, I'm sure.

It's so tiring, living. I will need rugs.

What kind of people display fake fruit for guests?
Welcome, and remember the hunger that
          can never be filled.
A face can do the same work without the worry
          of dust.

Here's a list of three things I'll fail to do:
          enjoy life
          overthrow the government
          record an album of songs about monsters

If I work very hard and forgo all enjoyment,
          someday, I'll still be broke and miserable
          but in a different pair of shoes.

When there's no change to be had, people
          pretend it's the janitor's fault they've
          left trash everywhere.

Sometimes, if you throw yourself under the bus,
          the bus drags you home. This is as close
          to a new life as many of us could afford.

Whose turn is it to stack the dishes in the sink?
I'm supposed to tell you to be grateful for having a sink.

Eating the Sun

Who among us hasn't eaten the sun
just to hurry things up? An existential
palate cleanser. Outrunning
the wolves requires exceptional
hamstrings. And then what will they
eat? Sometimes, you have to take
the bad with the worse and be glad
there isn't pudding. Some people,
all they have is a vanity plate and
a list of demands no one will ever
read. Present company avoided.
It's not the fur that makes you sneeze,
it's knowing that nothing will ever
taste as good as your heart. I don't
mind sharing as long as you take
me dancing. Really, just a
glance in my direction every now
and then to keep me focused. A man
will walk into an empty room and
knock just so no one thinks he's
there for nefarious reasons. The truth
is, he's there for the candy dish.
The way footsteps on wood distract
from the slowing heart. I wonder if
the hardest part of getting the sun down
is knowing everything after will be
dark and cold, the wolves howling,
still able to track you by scent while
you stumble, arms thrown out, trying
to find something firm to rest against.

Ava Or Noah

We named you like we named the pets—
a transitory word that never stuck, so
if someone asked this one's name, we'd
say the nickname, the abbreviation,
and then the formal, tracing our relationship
from idea to surprise to loving. You

skipped from idea to grief. A Rorschach
of metaphors—miscarriage as marriage,
miscarriage as plans, miscarriage as hope.
It's a little thing, loss. A shining star
that draws the eyes into the darkness.

Bees

Bees duck into a crack at the base
of the stairs, one and then another
in formation like quiet schoolchildren.
My daughter is afraid they'll like

her too much. I want to say it's a good
problem to have, but she won't get
it. So I stand between her and them
until the man can come and usher

them to a new home. We're walking
to the mailroom so we can get
the book I ordered for her with money
I don't have. Don't waste your life

on stories, I want to say. "I'm ten,"
she says when I say anything I think
is profound. I don't mean reading.

I don't mean the way the leaves
are shoved aside by the breath
of the world above us. All I mean is
that life is for living. That's something

I never did until she was born
and I decided I liked her too much
to ever run away again.

Ersatz Chemistry

A meaningless topic of conversation,
a mostly believable laugh, various pitches
of *huhs*. Someone has found a really
exciting brand of butter. This is how
my days bleed out, dying in the soil. Mornings
are the hardest time of year. Don't think
too much about how you'll spend more
time with these people than with your own
family, your couch, whatever it is you love.
You have no reasonable choice.
A grownup learns to master the art of not
screaming in the elevator. How much time,
per week, do you put into thinking about
decorative soaps, a new recipe whose
ingredients you can't pronounce, the void
waiting outside those glass windows
into which we are throwing the precious
hours of our lives because it's the path
of least resistance?

Good Things

Everyone will tell you to wait, but
none of them will tell you to get
ready while you wait. Do some
stretches. Take a class on financial
literacy. Learn to be someone you
can stand. When love comes, it will
spill its coffee on your shirt in an
elevator, so always carry those
detergent markers for stains. You'll
be trudging along trying to be
thankful for the overdraft fees when
a leaf slaps you just right and your
eyes rest on someone who's just
dropped their book in traffic. Rush
to help them and hope to God it's
not *Atlas Shrugged*. All of this is
a lie, of course. Love comes as
they're lowering her into the grave.
As he pulls the door quietly behind
him, wishing you good luck next
time. As the sun shadows over their
heads while they hold hands
somewhere you've never been.

Bus Stop Monster

The monster sat down on the bus station
bench, making it shake slightly. It caught
my eye, and we exchanged nods. Its head,

ducked low under the bus stop awning.
I wondered how it slid under here, but
I'd been staring at my phone, waiting

for something to happen. Here it was.
The monster was covered in orangish
fur, like a big tabby cat. Its features

were exaggerated—big bulbous nose,
puckered lips, bulging eyes, its
head about a third as big as my whole

body. It wore a business suit, a nice
one. It looked tailored or at least fit
really well. The monster carried a tiny

briefcase—or, a regular sized one that
looked tiny in its paws, which had hairy
knuckles and looked like they could palm

my whole head. Looking at it made my
heart race. I wanted to ask it—well,
as soon as I thought of one question,

another popped up. Where was it going?
How did it intend to fit on the bus? Who
made that suit? What's in the briefcase?

Was it going to eat me? Was that speciest?
Was it wrong to think of it as a monster?
Did that make me the real monster?

Could I take a picture of it? The bus trundled
to a stop in front of us. The monster rose,
nodded back to me, and threw itself into

the door hole. It was pretty thick, but it
squeezed through. The whole bus shook
and listed to the side. I saw it negotiating

with the driver, who finally waved it on.
The bus shook with each step as it moved
toward the back. The driver was watching

it in the mirror. When the monster glanced
at me. I waved. I don't know why. The driver
shook his head and closed the door.

The bus pulled away. I was left on the bench.
It took a little while for me to realize that
was my bus and I was going to be late, now.

Footnotes on Your Disappearance

Your hair under my shirt. Air dented
by a missing presence. Lingering
pheromones in unexpected places.
Was I cooking in here or in love?
When I see you again and you say
you're doing fine, don't lie with
your eyes, argue with your boyfriend
when you think I'm out of earshot.
Just be fine. We gave each other so
much, there should be some left
to take with. There's a book
graspable only in certain lights
that lists the names of all we'll
never touch again. But the dead
don't die just to ease our days.
They say when you love someone
they're with you always. This, too,
can be a curse. They say men look
for their mothers in other women.
So maybe it's my fault you were
broken and fading, while I held
your hand and tried to think
of something nice to say.

How to be Alone

I always thought paisley was a foreign
cuisine that tasted like sunset over
a city I'd never see. I was wrong
about that but not the affordability
of plane tickets. An imperfect education
punctuated by bouts of seclusion
and drug use. I was wrong to think
everything could be swallowed if you
keep your head tilted up. When the silence
comes, nobody checks its ID before
letting it in. We sit and we wait and we
try not to move too much. It's so easy
to break things by nudging them out
of place, without even meaning to. It's so
easy to let the ruin know your name.
I thought I'd surrounded my heart
in wood, but you trained termites just
to show me. Now, everything gets in
and I've gone to bed from the chill.
I've learned so much from you. Argyle
isn't a color. Up isn't a direction on
a street map. All the people I thought
were a bad time were, no matter how
much you defended their music choices.
You cried once, early on, saying I'd
never love you as much as you loved me.
I guess I proved you wrong.

Capital T Truth

It's hard to tell what's true, especially
when there's so much to learn. A man
steps on a thorn, which is gingerly removed
and bandaged while his stinking foot rots
off. A woman falls into a river and is revived
by a delicious chicken soup enema. The rich
are given more money so that the poor
will live better lives, cheered by the untouchable
gold statues where the free hospitals used
to be. It's not just in Kansas. But at least Kansas
knows it's Kansas. The easier life gets,
the harder it seems. People just want
to be filled by something that doesn't dissipate
when the breeze changes. The warm lump
of assurance in the gullet, something to grind
the days against. Someone told us we deserve
it. Someone else said we didn't. All
of it is killing us a little bit, but never mind.
Our bodies will make good fertilizer someday.

In the Cut

Sometimes, Dad would turn over an arrowhead,
but never when I was with him. My brother
found half a grinding stone but lost it when

the house burned. My sister's meth-head ex
took Dad's arrowheads. We walked the fields
checking for blight, places to water or spray.

Or I rode beside Dad over burned fields,
the tractor's vibrations cancelling out any
speech. I wonder if he was just lonely. He

rarely spoke or acknowledged my running
commentary. I mostly tried to stay out of the way.
He eased along empty highways, the horizon

bluer than any water I'd ever seen. It was all
waiting; for rain, for the next field to slide into
view, for the unsatisfying lunch of Vienna sausages

or potted meat on stale Saltines, for Mom's slow
death to be over.

Jupiter

If I pulled all my chromosomes out
and lined them up, they would reach
to Jupiter, someone posted on social
media. What I want to know is: what
is your cat doing right now? My co-
worker said she was late to work
because of the protests, even though
they were in a different city. What I
wanted to say was: tell me more about
your dog, Butter, who eats off human
plates and drinks only bottled
water. She leaves on two TVs for him.
I'm beginning to think she doesn't
want to be here any more than me.
My phone rings when I'm trying
to pretend to be busy. It's someone who
isn't who they claim to be, which could
be said of all of us. I ask them about their
pets, hunched down in the bathroom so
no one will see me. They hang up, and
I'm left there to wash my hands on
the way out so no one can post a story
about me later. If I pulled all my
chromosomes out and lined them up
to Jupiter, I'd run up them and never
come back. I'd take your pets with
me. You have been warned.

Friday Nights

Those bottles of Tvarski's cherry
vodka, Cisco Black Cherry, lost
under the creaky bed are so long

gone, their dust has sprouted corn
shoots. I wouldn't want to meet
the roaches mutated from living

in their hardening interiors. Tell
me about the angels watching us, who
try to stoke the fires of rage to warm

us through the cold neglect. Did
they misplace their wings and take
the wrong bus? There's something

beautiful about the hard no, splayed
out like a drunk in an alley but under
neath this hot Arkansas sky. This

is a different kind of blue, burned
thin. It was fun because it had
to be, putting a name to our wasted

nights, but any of us would've traded
for hope faster than a white man
um actually's. Everything's grown

over, now, and stinks differently.
Those young bodies that never
creaked are somewhere under

the tangle trying to make a bitter joke.
I can remember all of your parents'
phone numbers, but not the name

of the first girl whose heart I broke.

Mary Oliver

I'm supposed to tell you a story
to make you forget how sad it is
you're going to die without having
enjoyed most of your life. Well, okay.
Nature is a good start, like how these
little gray birds roll in the dust on
a path outside my apartment, avoiding
the broken glass, stray cats. They do
it because their bodies make too much
oil, which is good for helping them be
aerodynamic, but not when it's too much.
This is a metaphor for how adaptations
often overwhelm our lives. But it's also
about birds, so Mary Oliver can eat it.
But not really, because she's really good,
if you're the kind of person who can
afford a garden. I still need a joke, though.
They're hard, especially in poetry, which
is supposed to be too pretentious to laugh
at itself. Here's one my daughter is working
on:
Knock knock.
(Who's there.)
Doorbell repairperson.
(Doorbell repairperson who?)
Ding dong.
She's still working on it. She's eight.
Don't be so fucking judgmental.

Just Say Yes or Nothing or Whatever You Like

I like your hair long, like memory
got lost and set up camp. Like time
is learning how to play guitar, but
is mostly just jamming on stuff it
made up, right now. It has high
hopes of taking lessons. This is
where I live, now, between the honey
and apple, the soft sandalwood
that I swear is whispering my name.
It's probably all a terrible misunderstanding
that will lead to apologies and tears.
But for now, something like being
swaddled and struggling to breathe.
No one can tell me any different
without a warrant. I don't know
the true name of this place, but
I will call it home, if you let me.
There's a kind of darkness that
never lets in any light. The real end
of day, streaming behind us like a
"Just Married" sign. You can make
a home for yourself, here, also, in
the quiet place, where nothing can see
itself well enough to go wrong. I don't
presume to put needs in your mouth.
All of us are just looking for some place
to sit down without feeling guilty
about it. The phone is always ringing,

but there's never anyone on the other
end. Probably Death got a wrong
number. Got to get up and check that
the pot isn't boiling over, the ceiling
isn't too tired of holding up the sky,
the floor isn't so dirty they can track
your footprints if you ever stopped long
enough to look down. I would sweep it
for you so you could spread out. None
of this is a way of saying anything other
than hello. But that doesn't mean anyone
is listening. All the teeth in the world part.
They just want to remind us they're here, too.

Koans

Death arrives on time when traffic
is light. A way of seeing that isn't
dependent on corporate sponsorship.

The best way to absorb a map is from
below. It takes two feet working at
cross purposes to understand infinity.

Wave your hand in the air like your
heartrate isn't an issue. Starved for love
is a good solution for high cholesterol.

Everything in its place is the funeral
director's creed. Dirt doesn't speak
the way we'd like to hear.

A certain kind of shame perched high
on the shoulder. A half-remembered name
that would've echoed through the night.

Something big is finally landing outside.
Learn the night's name so your letters
won't be returned to sender.

The dragon that eats the sun has
eyes bigger than its stomach. This is why
the Earth survives until dawn.

It isn't so much the weight of air as
the cost of hair gel. If you dance like
no one's watching they can still hear.

A campaign of slow attrition of the heart
takes too long to bear. If you don't stop
smoking I'll set you on fire.

To be humbled by truth is another
way of bowing. As if gravity weren't
humbling enough.

Just Ask the Smartch

I have to strangle a Dutchman.
It's not my choice, but it will
help the economy. Questions
of hand placement, the best way
to exit this bathroom stall. What
to tell his grieving bank account.
The boot needs a chlorine treatment.
It's the only way to be sure. Your
neck will thank me as soon as it
can catch its breath. If it doesn't,
that's a sign of poor breeding.
I have to tell the man with two
names a secret. Something about
the lack of agency, if that's okay.
I've found a plaque carver who
works cheap. I'm so tired of
crying in the darkness while
the darkness laughs. It's just
rude. And who is sharing the joke?
If everyone reading this gave
just $10, it would pay for me
to be able to see a positive bank
balance again. Think of the children.
Or the elderly. Or the people whose
names start with Q. I would give
the apple back to Eve with my thanks.
I would refill the Matterhorn below
cost. I would part the aglet and none
would be the wiser. Before it's too

late, I need to take a piglet to
the porcupine factory. They're having
a sale on gas-station sushi. I'm not
the one who drowned a thin-legged
smartch. I was busy rinsing
the heavens. Sometimes, I think
they'll never come clean.

August 20, 1934

I've been confusing flowers
with hummingbirds, the way each
flutters in the breeze, the quick
wings and the quick wearing down
of the body. I don't know either's
name, but I'm glad to see the dart
of color drowning out the neighbors'
stereos. There is so little to say
about light, and yet so much has been
said. It's more about the feeling
than the describing. The same is true
of anything with wings. This isn't
the morning you made, the flowers
you wanted to plant in the pasture,
the birds crying beyond the yard.
It's the imperfections in a thing
that make it valuable, loss that makes
love. None of this is a way of saying
I miss you, because light, it's more
about surrounding than bearing up.

Birds in the Graveyard

Something to understand about life
is that when you describe the birds
you heard chattering as your mother

died, a cousin or a stranger will argue
that they were squirrels or a different
species of bird or maybe they were

cars on their way to church. You can show
them pictures, produce field recordings,
it doesn't matter. Reading this, you're

thinking I'm saying that people are
the worst. What I'm saying is that
the birds in this poem meant well,

but none of us realized they were just
trying to find a mate, some food,
and they were probably made up

for poetic effect anyway.

Breakup Poem

I never loved you. You tell me
that's okay, and you feel the same,
but nothing would make you this
angry except the dangling modifier
of a heart. It's okay to wince
at that one. I'm just trying
to lighten the mood. You'd rather
hold on to this idea that you're
somehow the only one of us
walking around not covered
in shit. Honey, I can smell it in
your eyes every time you glance
my way. What I mean is that
you need to try harder. If you want
to stab me in a way I'll notice,
blunt your blade real good. Dig
around with it in the chest. Did you
know that rats, when they bite, spread
their two front teeth apart to open
the wound? It leaves you sore inside,
along with the bleeding. Do something
like that. You've got more pride than
a rat, haven't you? It would take
a lot of attention to find something
about me I don't already know
and hate. Am I worth the time?
Maybe it would be better spent trying
to find something interesting to do
with yourself. If you succeed, don't
tell me. That would be the sweetest
revenge.

Breakfast Plans

Michael worked from home, today,
which means bacon and eggs and naan.
I've spoken to him before about
the truth of wheat toast, but he remains
unconvinced. All of us sing in our
own ways. For some, it's a dirge.
For others, a call to eat.
Steph invited E and I to breakfast
Saturday with her and Donna. We'll
be in the middle of packing, which
means yes, of course, at the bougee
French place over where all those
rich people's kids live. It was Steph's
birthday recently, which means I've
got to bring a gift. I know the perfect
book, but it's already packed. The real
problem is I've done too good a job
of gift-giving in the past. When you do
things, people expect you to keep doing
them. They say life is all about baby
steps, but tell that to the bank. The shattered
egg has to put himself back together. Do
you really think a bunch of horses
and bureaucrats will help? Mostly, they'll
try to assign blame and then leave
on break. This is the way of bureaucracy.
When E was little, she didn't even crawl.
She scooted, hand up to grab the world.
I would like to say I'm not worried.

Digging for Magic Beans

Goodness is another excuse
to do evil and sleep well,
after. It's all a matter of color
coordination and needlepoint,
convincing the tiger to settle
for bean sprouts, the giant,
that magic beans don't
exist. When it all gets too
loud, you can either try to out-
scream the noise machines
or dig out your ears. Yes,
it's not fair. Yes, it's not
nice. A man walks from end
to end of the great hall, folder,
in hand. He has all the answers
to sustain you. As his feet
thicken and his legs tire,
he passes door after door, all
closed. Behind each, the new
world celebrates itself without us.

Lorem Ipsum

I never know what to say when the sky
cries about its ex-boyfriend dating
again. I, too, have felt loneliness almost
every day of my life, but no one wants
to hear that except a therapist and for
the same reason—it means you're probably
not shutting up any time soon. What to do about
the way moonlight pools in someone else's
eyes? I signed a contract with the sun,
but you can't stop third party distributors.
No one—not even the sky—wants to hear
words like gloaming, and yet I can't flip
through a dictionary without finding it.
The problem with dystopias is someone
is always going to ruin it by being happy.
That's what people do: whatever you think
they won't. All of this means the sky
has moved on to someone who doesn't
make everything about themselves but
instead focuses on it, like they're supposed
to. Sometimes, being a good friend means
seducing the sky's ex and breaking their
heart. Try not to fall in love. That's all
any of us can do.

Mother, Father, Son, Daughter

The devil's biggest problems are lack
of dopamine. Nose-blindness. Not
existing. One expects time to pass,
some progression to be revealed,
not this dog-trying-to-stand-in-a-
pickup thing we've got going on.
First, there was the mother. Then,
the father, trying to erase the memory
of the light from her eyes, soothing
fingertips on fevered brow. Finally,
the son who forgot his keys and had
to run back home for them. It probably
all has to do with prisms because I
was absent that day. There are people
who spell out their pettiness onto signs
and stand outside places to try to
intimidate others. There are people
who walk into schools with automatic
weapons and open fire. There are
people who sit in pews one day a week
and think that's enough to make them
people. It wasn't that long ago a person
could be murdered for asking questions.
Even still, questions are met more
often with shame than considerations
of where the answer might come from,
and who. The son—it's his age, remember—
thinks crystals will save him or maybe
just yelling at the wall until it feels
punched. There's a fourth age no one
seems to have considered: the daughter.

Polar Bear

There's a polar bear in my pants. No.
I mean there's a polar bear wearing
my pants, walking around the office.
He grumbles like everyone else,
bumping the bathroom door open
with his rump to keep from touching
it. Drinking bureaucracy in like stream
water. We had to prop the breakroom
doors open to get the smell of nuked
seal and elk out. Steve asked where
the bear's unicycle was, and they
transferred him to another department
over in Rensen building. I didn't train
the bear to wear my pants; I taught
him to talk and write cursive, but
the pants thing he learned himself.
I thought, what could it hurt? I thought,
the ice is melting, what can I do to help?
It was the only vacation I took this year,
except for the one where I stayed in bed
for a week. I trudged to the unbridled
wastelands of the north, which is what
I call my living room, then I caught
a cheap flight to the arctic circle. It wasn't
hard to find a polar bear looking for work.
There were a bunch of them hanging
out in front of the building supplies store—
some local place I'd never heard of. I hid
him in my luggage because I didn't have

a clue where to get a passport up there.
He said, "Hey Cort, Cortorino, how about
you get me some scrumptious seal cakes?
I'm starving." It's true. He was thin
as hope. All I could find were these fish
sticks that'd been recalled for having seal
in them. It was on all the news shows.
"I'm going to get you on your feet," I told
him as he gulped them down. I taught him
to hurry up and wait, to smile through
the sadness and talk to strangers about
the weather. His whole family had starved
to death the summer before. It wasn't hard.
When my place advertised an opening, he
applied with the resume we'd made. "I wanted
to surprise you," he said. "You sure look
surprised."

Julius

I found the source of the cold
spot in the wall. It was a dead boy.
Don't worry—long, long gone.
Something had torn the plastic
open, letting the bones mold over.
He said his name was Julius,
which he knows is a nice name.
"How long have you been in here?"
I asked. "Since I died," he said.
I don't think it was meant as
a joke. The thing is, I'm concerned
not only about my deposit—for
the hole I put behind the stove—
but for the press this is going
to lead to. I'm trying to keep
things laid back. Julius said
he doesn't miss his family
anymore. He saw their lights
flash as each ascended, leaving
him here. "Do you know who
killed you?" I asked. His eyes
darkened. The room went
cold. "You did," he said.
"I'm pretty sure I'd remember
that," I said. He laughed.
"I'm just messing with you."
I had a lot of questions, but
I wasn't sure how to proceed.
I put on some cartoons and made

a list. "Do you have any super
powers?" I called from the kitchen.
"Just the light flashing/cold thing,"
he said. "Can you read minds
or anything?" he shook his head.
Bits of ectoplasm splattered onto
my couch. I wished I'd thought
to put down towels. "Can you
predict the future?" I asked,
"Or solve crimes?" "No,"
he said. "I can do this, though."
I rushed in to see him make
it look like he pulled the tip
of his thumb off. "Eh?"
he said. I went back to the kitchen,
and scratched that off my list.

Mornings, Feeding the Fish

There was a different smell in the morning.
The cows were quiet. The breeze

came in from the Lake down the hill.
The sun hadn't heated the dead

fish, yet. You could believe the world
was new, just because it hadn't

seen light in a while.

Pulling Coffee Weeds

Pollen is just another kind of lust
in the air, which shows that everything

wants the same thing. I remember,
that day, not wanting to sit between my

brother and father and listen to
them bicker anymore, both of them

stunted in ways I couldn't understand
yet. It was that old blue dodge

Dad drove for more than
20 years until somebody drove it

off a cliff. They set me out, my brother
saying it was too much for me,

and me wanting to be free and clear
not only of their words but the

stickiness of childhood. I took
a small scythe and set to cutting

thick coffee weeds in a soybean field.
They left me, took the water and

I imagined the breeze. Later, when
I'd cleared the field, another man

came with his grandson to shoot
cans. The gun was bigger than

the boy; he had to hold it between
his knees, hunched over. I got

yelled at for suggesting this might
not end well. Men sprawling in

the dying heat, their hackles up
from frustrating work, guns and

beer. I drank in the stink of it all,
trying to find something in it
I didn't already know.

Poem with Tiger Lilies and Dust Jackets

The tiger lilies on the side of the road
have died back in the heat, so I'm not
sure why I'm still coming to work, except
that it's where I keep my oatmeal. I don't
know what to do for breakfast, otherwise,
except hit the drive through and feel sick
and useless all day. Let me tell you what's
wrong with your dust jacket pics. You don't
know shit about life. That's the whole point
of being a poet. The knowing smile, the smug
condescension. Show yourself confused
at a four-way stop, and I'll buy your book.
Show yourself lost and stupid when
they leave your selfish ass, and I'll applaud
when you smile sheepishly and pause
at the coffee shop. You can't win poetry,
no matter how many awards you throw
at it. Your teacher or someone just like him
is judging the thing. You're not fooling
anyone but yourself. I smile in mine, but
I'm embarrassed by my teeth. I can't afford
to get them fixed. If you don't know
that's poetry, I can't help you.

Sorrow All Around

I saw my landlord sitting on the curb,
crying. All around him, people were
toting their belongings to the backs
of pickup trucks, piling them into
the street where traffic already honked
around them. "No one cries for me,"
he said, his nose big and red, his eyes
dead. I tried to be cautious around
him ever since he caught me trying
to fit into a bird's nest in a tree. He
stood under me and asked what I
was doing. I said I just wanted to
know what it felt like to be an egg.
"I'm not liable," he said and shook
the tree. I broke my collarbone when
I fell. He made me pay for the concrete
that was already cracked, even though
I didn't fall on it. I'm pretty sure it was
his boot that ruined my nose, but he
wouldn't admit it. "What happened?"
I asked. "I have feelings," he said. I
didn't believe him. "To them," I said,
pointing. He shrugged. He was sitting
right in the way of several of them,
sobbing loudly. I decided that if anyone
came by carrying a piano, I'd trip them
right over his head. I tried to pass him,
but he shifted so I had to step around.
"No walking on the grass," he said.

"Then move," I said. That's the kind
of thing that gets your rent raised, but
I was tired from working two jobs that
day, just to afford living there. "You're
just like them," he said. "You don't care
about who I am inside." I had no choice
but to stand and watch him. It's the kind
of thing that happens when you've made
the regrettable decision not to be born rich.
Nobody's fault but my own. "No one
cries for me," he said again. "You've made
plenty of us cry," I said. "Which is close
to the same thing." That satisfied him enough.
He wandered away. I went inside to the mice
and noise. Another wasted day. Another
lost night.

Morning Ministrations

I can't sleep on this new medication,
so I go down to the dirty river's edge
near my apartment, before the traffic
makes me too fearful to be on foot.
The air shines as the morning light
reflects on particles I probably shouldn't
be breathing. There's trash, a Starbucks
cup no snail would claim, moss on
the gravel that reminds of the rind on hot
chocolate, but green. Bugs dance over
the water, spelling out a calligraphy in
the air. Dragonflies hover, feeding, just
like they did back home when Dad would
take me out on the Lake to feed the fish,
early mornings while he was still sober.
I would skip a stone, if I remembered how,
but I don't want to disturb the bugs,
the water, the quiet before the morning
is subsumed. So, I stand, just back from
the mud. Past the far shore, up on the road,
cars pass quietly every few minutes. Under
the bridge, off to the left, homeless people
are rousing to find a place to clean
themselves and get to work. One of them
watches as I watch the water.

Spring

Spring slips in, full of questions. When
did the fire sneak from the sky to rest
in this ditch, disguised as the hidden
faces of tulips? The worms are keeping
a secret about what dreams misplaced
taste like. Everything beautiful grows
from something someone forgot to do.
The most devastating damage is done
in the name of expediency. People
have searched their whole lives, huddled
in filth, for the secret, when the birds
had it all along. They're singing about it,
if you listen. The song says: come
stay with me for a little while.

Some Thoughts on Moonflowers

Skitterings in the night, like
    bristly feet and dripping teeth.
    I am not butter, I don't
    care what the pamphlets say.
    You may not fry anything in me.

Magic lacks melatonin, which
is why it hides from the sun.
Ask anyone who knows.
Shadows. Moving lights.
If all the evil could shut
the fuck up that would be
great. I'm trying to die, here.

My head hurt for days because
    I couldn't afford to keep up
    with my meds. Don't tell me
    it's about anything other than
    greed.

It's always raining somewhere
    n mi hart. *tap tap*

Maybe the mice are putting on a symphony.
Maybe the moonflowers are going for a walk.
Maybe the dust bunnies are thirsty for blood.

When I go on meds, I can't see anything
    inside my head, so I have to write
    to have thoghts.

It's about keeping myself safe because
  the squeaky wheel gets evicted.

On a scale of one to ten tell me how
  Capitalism is treating you today.
  The first two don't count.

These nights when I'm waiting to be
  recycled, I think about the warmth
  of your body in my arms
and remember there was a time
    however brief
  I didn't feel alone.
haha no take backs.

Remember the Lightning and Her Sister Darla

Back then, the world existed in 4-minute slices,
radio friendly, and capable of being shined
with the right spit. We never listened to
the words because we trusted the censors, not
realizing they were dying like the rest of us.
Pastries tasted like sugar, and funny colors
didn't matter in a beverage. This morning,
I dumped out my leftover intentions in
the parking lot so I could recycle the cup. Maybe
a flower was trying to grow from that concrete.
I followed a man to the stairs—give me
the confidence of an old man in shorts
and sandals, black socks worn without irony,
and an overwhelming need to chat with strangers.
I was never that unable to question others' desire
for my company, and I have mania. Inside,
everything is animal, including my shirt. Every
day, I forget the color of the sky until I sneak
out and ask someone. Most times, they look
from one to the other and shrug. I finally
petitioned to get a screen put up. It flashes "blue
and sometimes gray" from dawn until dusk.
I still ask because I don't like to believe. Back
then, the sky was always forgetting me. Lightning
asked my name at parties, so it knew who to avoid.
Now, I see it on my morning commute. Ugly
tie and khakis. Sleeveless blouse the wrong
color for its skin. Its sister Darla got married

and divorced a long time ago. She's back
from the coast, but no one seems to know
which one. Kids and debt. When I catch the last
elevator with the lightning, it's shaking its head,
shocked at the state of things, like us all.

The Enemy of My Enemy Is Probably Also My Enemy, Just Without a Goatee.

For example, no man can wear beige
and remember the taste of the sun. Look,
Jim, just because you went to private

school doesn't excuse you from a responsibility
to understand physics. It doesn't matter how
good you look in lacrosse shorts when they

come to reclaim the fields. Sweat soured
on skin like a father's gaze. A bell that never
stops ringing. I want to laugh like we used

to, talking shit about the pines. Maybe
you're right, Jim. Maybe there's nothing
but quiet cars. The flimsy logic of regret.

There's a certain way of forgetting
that happens every night when you try
to catalogue what remains. It has to do

with never going into the kitchen,
which is the best way of keeping
the floor clean.

The Whitest Fish On the Hook

It's a kind of ache, though I'm not
supposed to say. But it's okay if
you don't listen. Imagine the dust
doesn't taste like corpses, the sky
isn't a traitor to us all, its red fingers
of incandescence trailing the small
of your back like you can't smell it
on its breath, its hard eyes. Intention.
But maybe it's not the dust's fault. It
is what it is, born underfoot from
the corpses of those who tread upon it.
The softest shovel for the most delicate
game. We expect it to know better
but none of us is willing to teach it.
Nobody taught us, we say, except all
those who did. The tongue is the biggest
class traitor since electricity. Touch
it and see it recoil from your blood-
stained hands. Who among us hasn't
begged the bee to sting us rather than
let us eat its children? What am I
supposed to do in the evenings other
than weep at the lives of those who will
always have more than me? Maybe I'll
learn a hobby. Big man with a drug habit.
No one thanks desolation for clearing
out the rubes. You're still not listening,
right? Good. This is the part where I
slip in all my secrets about how to deal
with the ache without angering the shovel,
the dust, the spaghetti sauce-clogged ears.

Pollen-Covered Parchment

I've been slipping notes into the budding
petals of the volunteer tulips in your back
yard. If you discovered them when
the dog you got to replace me chewed
the stalks bare and spit out their bones,
it was me. I trained bees to carry them
in exchange for space inside my barbed-
wired-off hive. (Someone has to save
the planet.) My tiny scribbles, meticulous
as lies, detailing my feelings with footnoted
failures, ideas for perpetual motion machines
powered by loss, the secret names of the unloved
dying. Listen, all of this is a game we're born
bored of. Neither of us needs joy when we've both
got cable. I'm sure you never bothered to rescue
them from the dog's mouth, as you never picked
up after it before I gave you back your key,
so this note you won't read doesn't
even matter. I'm sure all of this is a sign
of my own failure of imagination. It's just
that someday I hope to plant tulips. Daisies,
even. It would be nice if there was something
to them other than the faint smell of striving.

Night Swimming

I snuck out to swim the river
behind my apartment. Night slanted
across the surface, as if to say

this is ours and you are not us.
This isn't the first time I've had
to apologize to the night for

a transgression. Who, among us,
hasn't been seventeen and in love?
Something lifts its head above

the dirty water, my eyes thirsty
for anything other than desperation.
I threw a flower, which landed

in the center of a star. The thing
is, I was afraid to admit I never
learned to swim. But I could

wade—why don't you believe
me—I could wade like a son
of a bitch. Behind me, the dark

eyes of children's bedrooms.
I wanted, somehow, to wish
them safe. Things were done

to me I hope you never learn
the words for. But I can't even
struggle to the middle of this

crusty puddle without lights
flapping on, dogs yarping, someone
threatening to tell their husband

something is happening they
don't understand. "Shut up,"
I say, "No fucking takebacks."

Not one of them know what
it is to love or be loved the way
the moon ignores me.

Vertigo

But the world won't stop spinning
if you get thrown off. The gears
won't stop grinding if you fall into
their embrace. The trains will probably
be delayed, but that has nothing
to do with you unless you fell onto
the tracks. They don't even care enough
to get it right, is all. They just keep
going. Every day, it gets harder with
brief respites. You have a snack
to see you through until one day
you discover you can't catch your
breath after sitting down. This is what
you trained for, all those years.
Realize that a lot of somebodies lied
to you all your life. When you approach
the edge, are you going to stare like
a bird or step off like a man? I can't
tell you what to do with your time,
but have you considered that yoga
is just another name for God, as is donut,
bad luck, or Capitalism. So when
I say yoga is dead, please understand:
no one gives the slightest bit of a fuck
if you're offended by the sight
of yourself in someone else's mirror.
There are habits we learn when there's
nothing else to sustain us. You've got
to put your fist through the brick

wall of sustainability. You've got to
choke comfort out and then run away
from its corpse before somebody
calls the cops. Staring at the void
isn't going to do anyone any good.
Plumb the depths and write a travel
brochure. Make friends with the
bottom feeders. How are they
any worse than your landlord?

Everything Ends Badly, Otherwise It Wouldn't End,
after a line by Christopher Fullerton

It's hard to describe the weather when
the sunset keeps salivating behind your back.
A type of rodent that sheds its fur and learns
to yodel has some interesting things to say about
predetermination and your mother. The only
difference between a sunset and sunrise
is a handful of letters and several hours. Also,
you can't see after one and you don't want to
after the other. A certain amount of filler allowed
in each heart. A certain amount of negotiation
before each separation. There are certain species
of flies that are born and die in a single day. I bet
some of them begrudge it taking so long.

Doing the Work

My therapist thinks being
polite is the same as faith,

smile. This is how we
patronize each other, her

promises not to burn me
from the ground up. With her,

many has always been my
problem. That's not the right

I never woke up alone, but
I never slept, either. Let me

Edward G. Robinson voice)
Meow, see, meow. My daughter

To put it another way,
if I open my mouth, what do

tongue, which   is another way
of saying writer's block, the

through the nests, looking
for the sound of my own

approval. When I was a boy,
and the sickness took her, my

listening to the animal
that had gotten in, waiting

a habit, worn long enough—
like a crate-trained soul—I

and me and God. If I promise
to jump at the thunder, He

it's just cash. She asks if
I have any friends. I say too

word. What I mean to say is
that when I was younger,

tell you a joke. What does
a gangster cat say? (In an

and I made that up together.
Maybe you had to be there.

you think will come out? Dirt
daubers crawling on my

smell of mud, which is another
way of saying death. But I paw

voice before I lost the accent,
the mud for my father's

mother would howl late into
the night, me lying in the dark,

for it to find me and feed. I'm
not trying to complain. Lots of

my friends had much harder
lives than I until they died. She

I'm going to kill myself,
but I can't today; I have an

somehow to last that long. Not
that I'm implying in any way

for her so obviously practiced
sincerity; the last thing I need

I've tried to die. Water, wind,
a bullet's kiss, the things of

can barely stand. This is why
I don't own a gun. Do you drink

the world I'm not prepared
to take, I say. The only thing

could've saved her, I could
forgive myself for still being

forget to be angry. Let's not
talk about me anymore. She

your trauma. When that's
done, I want you to run as far

or soothe yourself in some
way. I can hear rain outside

asks why I'm here, and I say
I'm buying time. I'm tired.

appointment. Give me a decade.
Help me find the strength,

that it would be your fault.
She nods, and I'm grateful

is to fling a craving on some
body. Here is a list of ways

the world I've swallowed. I've
got so much going for me, I

or do drugs? She asks. That's
a kind of trust exercise with

I remember about my mother's
smell is urine. Maybe, if I

alive. But forgiveness is
a myth; eventually, you just

says, Okay Here's an exercise.
I want you to write about

away from it as you can.
And then have a snack

as I type this, working on its
aim. Maybe I'll order pizza.

The Ocean Comes Home

It's just past noon, and the world
has slowed its ending long enough
for us to catch our breath and keep
it in the most intricate gilded cages.
The darkness in the sky tastes of copper.
When the clouds drop their loads,
the ocean will creep into our noses,
carrying its rough cloth rucksack,
and begin to spread its things. It's
important to be comfortable. That's
something the jagged mountains never
understood. A throw rug to dampen
the echoes. A reading lamp to warm
the napping chair. It may not ever
be early afternoon again. Someone
in the hallway is screaming, tears
rushing down to get away from
the braying goat noise. The salty
mountain of the ocean floor opens
its eyes and blinks. What it sees
is better than fish but doesn't talk
as much shit, either. The ocean
closes its blinds. It's had as much
peopling as it can stand. The world
jerks back into motion. All of us
get back to the busy job of dying.

Fire from the Sky

They came on a Wednesday. It was raining.
I had to get my car inspected. The first
thud shook the building. I went to the window;
my coworkers didn't move. Arcs of fire stretched
from mid-sky to the ground. I watched them
hit, some knocking holes in buildings full
of people. Some punching into pavement,
sidewalks. I don't know why I went outside.
Curiosity, I guess. Nothing interesting ever
happened at work. But as I huddled in the
entranceway, one slammed into the building,
above me. I ran into the street. Cars careened
around me, each other, the holes newly opening.
I suspected this was a dream, but other than
the falling stones, nothing else was strange.
No clowns with chainsaws for arms. No strange
women I'd known forever but never met. One
hit the parking deck, and I raced to my car.
I was the first one out, so I made it down
and outside. I realized I couldn't see the sky
that way, so I pulled into a parking spot and got
out. They were stones, falling, on fire. I'd always
heard they broke up in the sky. Maybe these
were so big, these were the pieces. Maybe they
were somehow too hard to break up. I saw
a woman disappear before she could even scream.
Just a hole in the sidewalk. My lunch break was
almost over. I didn't know which way to go.

Dream Woman

I dream about a woman I've never met.
When I wake up to pee, I come back
to find her smirking in a different room.

She's sick in a way she won't explain.
There's wind howling outside the way
it did on that lonesome house on a hill,

rain trying to tear its way in. We said
it was witches scratching their fingernails
on the bricks, but it's old white men

trying to kill people over hairdos. I learned
that a long time ago. But maybe if I knew
the secrets of cats—which are mostly

just what they've killed recently and where
it's hidden. It's not every night this
woman needs my help, but won't say

how. I've trained my whole life for this.
She's getting prettier, the older I get.
I wish I could say the same. Her eyes

are an exhale, softer than they used to be,
and her lopsided smile is warmer, tinged
with the pain of waiting but also hope.

If I don't meet her soon, I'm afraid neither
of us will be able to help the other. I'm sure
this is me being selfish, somehow. I'm sure

I'm doing something wrong.

Come Sit Beside Me and Have Some Funyuns.

I'm learning how to make a cat's
cradle. Just let me borrow your hand
for a little while. Sometimes, it's like
something bad is going to happen
if I have to drag you all out into the street
and make it happen. My friend said
my life isn't boring compared to other
people. I said I don't compare myself
to other people. My other friend said,
"Prague will change your life." I said,
"Bitch, I can't make rent." Going to Prague
would still be boring "me," but homeless "me"
when I got back. I can't light myself
on fire to sit on the couch and watch
Whose Line Is It Anyway? reruns. I don't
even remember the smell of smoke.

The Stone Carver Has Dirty Nails

It's surprising we haven't fallen into the sky
like the clouds before us, siphoned from

a surplus of forgotten history and hanging
out. They wait in case someone remembers

something someday, which is the primary
purpose of math. To make the perfect mixed

drink requires breaking a few hearts. Our
ancestors died so that we'd have the right

to have dead ancestors. Somebody had to
pay for all those gravestones, which means

wealth doesn't so much die with us as it's
passed on to the worms. There were days

when it was enough to stand or sit, teach
new dogs old tricks. We slept an amount

that didn't make healthcare professionals
shake their heads. Who can say who has

it worse when no one will shut up about
that sandwich they had that time, and why

does my toe hurt? I'm starting to think no
one is going to take me up on this plan to

build a whiskey still in heaven. All those
old halos not doing anyone any good. Fine.

This is why I'm the one who knows how
to have a good time and you're the one

everyone looks uncomfortable around. I'll
say it to his face if I have to, but I'll smile.

Fall

A laugh evaporating from the weeping
willow in my yard, a hiding
place for worms. Oh, Fall, let me finish
my book before you kill us all. I've
been flying through the chapters,
but you have to put that chainsaw
down. This bit is about love and this
bit is about cooking dumplings.
I'm happy to lie in the dirt if you'll
just get out of my light. My eyes are
stones. My eyes are jello shots. My
eyes aren't what they used to be.
The same could be said of absolutely
everything. Oh Fall, tell me your secret
plan for what you'll do with the bodies.
Your eyes are a broken cage the rat
long since escaped from. Your eyes
are really set off by that red dress.
When the rains come, we'll sell them
to California. Let's ride the bus humming
a song just quietly enough that no one
registers but everyone hears. They'll
be singing it in their heads for hours. Fall,
you were a queen, once, before the calendar
declared democracy. I will always love
you more than you let me. Hold my hand
while you cut it off. You sure look pretty
in that dress.

It's Nice to Know At Least One Person Understands Who I Truly Am and Hasn't Pressed Charges.

Life is hard and we're all tired. That's
why they promised us wings. What
a joke. The care and feeding of pinfeathers.
The cost of dry-cleaning, alone. Just try
finding a place that handles feathers with
an organic process. No one considers
having to sleep on their side forevermore.
Or those little bugs that live in the feathers,
and what kind of time commitment to
after-school activities they'll bring.
There are many kinds of addictions, but
this one is mine. Sometimes, I sit at my
desk, and I can taste the small deaths.
It's something with cheese melted on
and some kind of chocolate on the side.
I stayed an hour late because no one else
knows how to do anything. On the way
home, saw three cars slam into each other
trying to be the first to wait. Got home
nearly blind with ache, and there's a notice
that they might take my paycheck because
I'm not paying as much as they'd like.
It's enough to make a person do something
crazy like go to church or take up jogging.
I would be happy if the world would just
be quiet for a little while so I could cry
to myself without interruption. Maybe that's

not true. Maybe nothing would make me happy. But that doesn't mean it's okay to keep making me miserable out of convenience. What about my schedule? Don't I deserve the autonomy to decide when I'm thrown away, which specific cracks I'll slip through? I thought this was America.

Keep Going, I Guess

If I stop, I'll fall asleep: this is the secret
to adulthood nobody tells us. So much
of life is about hiding ourselves. If my nose
runs, people might figure out I'm human.
They'd never forgive me for that. Too
many humans have failed them. Name
something that isn't a metaphor for life.
Go ahead. I'll wait. But I might doze off.
The way we crush ants on the sink in
the bathroom. The complaining of cars
in the street. My best friend has rats,
and I can't handle mice. Living isn't
a competition, but it clearly is. I want to
say something about the way moonlight
makes things appear lovely, but it's really
the god of stubbed toes' only friend showing
off. When the sadness goes, you're left
with the fear that it'll come back. When that
eventually fades, boredom fills the void.
And anger over how much of your life
was taken by this disease most people make
fun of. The thing about snowflakes is no
one's actually measuring them, not really.
They just say that so your grandfather
feels better about himself. But why do we
care what grandfathers think about themselves?

Mud Man

Maybe I was made from mud—these
days, a man won't get much argument
saying that. The wet, sticky ball formed
in my momma's belly after she ate bitter
graveyard dirt to loosen that man's rope,
tugging on her heart. She had no sister
Betty to call out, "Stop! You'll only make
it tighter by fighting." But if they had, what
would it have mattered? She was hungry.
So, she brought her step-ladder to the bone-
field, saw nothing but drunkards and teenagers,
their barrel fires smoldering in the breeze,
and climbed over. Maybe that's why
I am the way I am, something in my skin
trying to get back to a long-dead life.
The great bank in the sky repossessed her
when I was young, so I can't ask anyone
who could answer. Mud, ashes to taste,
a restless heart wanting to be free of obligations.
My father worked the rice fields all his life,
shoveling mud into water that carried it
away. Plenty of it found its way to his lips,
but a man doesn't have the right spit.

My Teen Years in Mothballs

There were albums full of pictures of us
all dressed as characters from TV
shows we'd never seen. Quiet jealousy
over that one kid with all his toys
in their original packaging and what
that implies about the orderliness
of his bedroom. I'm thinking
about asking Melissa if I can go back
to that place where we talked politics
without knowing what it was to starve.
A team of professionals figured out what
was wrong with us: a lack of love
and opportunity, just like everyone
else, but we also wore plaid. We didn't
know how lonely we were until someone
asked us to dance. We'd cry and cry
on their shoulders, until they asked
the DJ to play something faster.

Once the Dogs Stop Barking

There comes a point when you have
to go down to the street, point your
nose to the river, and follow its bends

home. No one will stop for you to cross.
If you walk too far, you'll end up part
of the catfish's mystique. If there

aren't catfish, it's probably the wrong
kind of river for you. Let's be honest.
Make a list of all the things you'd cut

out of your heart, if you could, then sell
that online so you can afford a knife.
If no one wants it, substitute your under

wear. This is how you solve problems.
You can jot them as you walk. Find
a way to get past the bridges, the fences,

the gated condos with their walls. They
will absolutely call the cops if they see
you bleeding or being. Someone always

thinks they have something to say
that's worth listening to, but they never
want to pay the ASCAP fees. They call

this a consumerist culture, but you don't
have a choice as to who eats your corpse.
What horse shit. At the very least, you

can sell plasma, if you can get to the clinic.
It won't make rent but you can buy food
to replenish yourself. This is the world

we and our neighbors let happen. I'm
not trying to make waves. I just want
to go home, thanks.

The Dead Don't Speak Because Their Lips Are Sewn Shut

I never dream   of my father   but often
of his house.   He's already dead.   My mother
the ghost   I've always known.

My brother has some scheme   to not have to work
like the time   he started a rice field   by the Lake
to brew Budweiser knock-off beer   He trained crows
to pick the grains   individually   without eating them
He had to learn their language   They were his best friends

or the time he paved the pasture   and sold parking

My sister   is the only one with any sense
in my dreams.   She works a panini press
in the magic kingdom.   Someday   a prince will order
a turkey club   with a side of communication and mutual
respect

My ex-wife believed   my mother's ghost
watched over me.   I imagine her   floating
above my bed   wondering when   I'm going
to change these sheets

But is she   the wraith I knew   impossibly wearing
her wedding dress   or what they buried   her in?
Is she the dying   old lady the beauty queen
or the desiccating corpse?
Are her eyes glued shut?   Her lips sewn?

She urges me not   to look back.
The past is trauma   we're already well-versed in.
Look to the future devastation.

I've forgotten her voice.   Someday, I'll forget
my father's my brother's   Or maybe
I'll die before I forget.

This Is the Kind of Place You're Last Seen In

I want to find a shadowed dirt road,
the kind they made so many of when
I was a kid—that's why they're gone:
over-production. Bottom dropped out
of the market. It could be anywhere,
as long as it leads me nowhere slow.
Spindly oaks mixed with overconfident
pines shading the sides. Dust in the air
and the odd rock flying. Remember
when bugs smeared our windshields,
deer darted from the trees in their terrified
game of tag? I would drive it all night
without pulling over. I've seen too
much of the world not to sleep behind
a locked door. It's not that the woods
hide wolves, it's that they hide what
killed out the wolves. Maybe it would
lead to some old bridge where the kids
used to knock each other up and out.
Spray-paint all over so other wild
kids could remember them when they
get old, fat, and still broke. If I kept
going, would it take me to some old
town everybody forgot to leave and how
to get back to? Maybe it's haunted or
just full of meth cooks and raccoons.
Maybe I could move into a shanty
everyone before me has died in. My
apartment is too comfortable without
giving any comfort. I miss those days
of wind blowing through her hair.

Where Do You See Yourself in Five Years?

The man on the other side of the table
is a variety of sneezes, held together
inside beige by sheer force of lack
of will. What he's smelled out there
is more sensible than me, but I don't
so much fault him as marvel at his
restraint. In the face of all joy, this
man chooses the sour eye. He gets
excited at the prospect of a new tie
on Father's Day. His hair is a damp
smattering of crumbs from other
people's meals, and he's proud of
its pedigree—carries a laminated
copy. Everything about him is
something I don't understand, something
I would avoid at all costs, and vice
versa, but the difference is he holds
the soft feathers of my future in his
sweaty palms and all I hold is the bill.

Good Luck. I Hope You Get the Job.

You are not 23. You were never
23. Pretty eyes full of innocent
fear—the kind that haven't learned
enough to hide it. Skin smooth, all
the usual details no one really notices
until they're gone. Tell me about
the experience you have in sighing.
What about appealing to diverse audiences
who are mostly kind of sad inside
and sleepy? Apologize for coming
alive. Apologize for knowing the answer.
A nervous smile for the Good. A forced
chuckle for the Real. You can be the kind
of person who takes or the kind
of person who tells themselves they give,
but you can't choose. Maybe you're right.
I hope you are. Would you rather be
the flower unaware its scent was gasoline
or the ashes who know how to burn?
I wasn't always an avalanche. Once,
I perched like a crane above the world's
peacock feathers. What do you think it
got me? Even the smallest mouse knows
the taste of blood. We had one in the other
day who misspelled their own name. What
we do here is just like what everyone does
everywhere. Do you have any questions?
You really should before it's too late.

Instructions

1

When you wake, take
the morning's face in
your hands and breathe
into its lungs until
it remembers you. It won't
remember you. Light whispers
through the blinds
from someone else's
lamp. It's ok. They
won't ask for it back
as long as you're quiet.

*

Prayer is another way
of grieving, a plaintive voice
begging the electron to de-
nature. Either way, no one
is listening except your knees.

If you can't remember how
to rise, pretend you've died.
The shuffle on carpet
is a kind of funereal music.
The thought of it is enough
to fill you with something like
electricity; it jumps to leave you
the first chance it gets.

2

When you wash the night's
soil from your face, it won't
matter how hard you scrub;
the best you can hope for
is blood. When there's too
much to drain away, call
a plumber. This is how
the economy grows. Be
proud to contribute. Someday,
you'll feed the choicest worms.
Their children may
be president.

*

Nodding off in the shower
is the closest to being born
you'll get today. Someone
is knocking on the door, asking
for batteries, does this
match? Is my "I want"
song in key? Need
is the true name for love.
If you're not buying that,
there's probably something
wrong with your heart. Sorry.

3

When you eat, thank the testers
for the little deaths. This
is the way to make breakfast:
remember that you're special
because everyone is. Then,
add cheese. Bacon is probably
worth going to hell for, but that's
for God to decide. All you need
is a chorus, some toast, eggs,
and Duke's mayo. If you accidentally
glimpse the way you'll die,
go ahead and have orange juice.

*

We made hours to have something
to count, so dying is another
name for productivity. Clean
as you go so you have time to dread
later without distraction. Scotch
Gard your heart to reduce stains.

One finger points to the door.
The other points to the window.
Neither knows how to apply
for an NEA grant with anything
approaching success. If anyone
were watching you, they'd think
you were a fucking idiot right now.
Put your plate in the sink. Pull
up your pants. Wipe something off.

4

When you dress, hide
in the closet until the clothes
find you. This is the origin
of the saying, sometimes
you get the bear, sometimes
the bear gets your socks.
She said, the thing about you,
is no matter how dark it gets,
there's always a turn,
at the end. This was another way
of saying goodbye.

*

How would you like
to be judged? As the snake
that eats its own skin, or
the apple that's forgotten
its worms? Consider questions
of belt viability, seam magnetism,
if the wind blows east, will
this shirt preserve my hymen?
Or will I have to marry
another Republican to learn
to distinguish between ugly
ties? (Spoiler: they're all ugly.)

5

When you travel, pretend
you have the knees of a much
younger man. If it helps,
name him Jimmy. Everyone
loves and no one trusts
a Jimmy. Most people you'll meet
want you dead, but don't take
it personally. It's just
Capitalism, poor seat design,
something we don't talk about
that happened one time. No matter
how much they yell, don't look. It's
a trick to add you to a list. All of it
since the forceps yanked you free
was a trick.

*

The question to ask is why,
if you hate everything, are
you trying to save it with public
transportation and not setting
random buildings on fire?
A more useful question is how
can you set yourself on fire
when you've burned up or given
away all your fuel? Keep
your eyes down. No one
is watching you. Except
that one guy, in the corner.
That fucker's taking notes.

6

When you work, remember
that the hand you've taken
is the state's; the ring, a cuff.
Convenience is another word
for love. If karma were real,
we'd all be damned, along
with God and the well-wishers.
It's all just some call center in an Idaho
prison, anyway. They don't even make
minimum wage to deliver those
thoughts and prayers.

*

A postcard from the copy room.
A postcard from the broken stall
in the men's room.
A postcard from the crying station
under your desk.
A postcard from the null space
behind the printer.
A postcard from the eye of the cord
tangle.
A postcard from the smell of hand lotion.
A postcard from yesterday's lunch.
A postcard from the dust
that has learned enough speech
to complain.
A postcard from a three-ton stack

of wasted paper.
A postcard from office politics
that says: Wish You Weren't Here.

7

When you break, imagine
the sidewalk doesn't regret
its station. You are the only
one who isn't happy holding up
the light. The crows don't even
notice you enough to mock.
You need a new belt. Pick
up your feet for fuck's sake.
Assume the trees aren't there
to hide bodies. That's
what the medians are for.

*

Now, ask yourself a question: if
our lives are guided by the wind,
why do so few of us know how
to mend a sail? Another way
of asking this is: who was the first
to close their eyes in the face
of seeing too much, and the first
to widen them to absence? Now,
find that person and kick their ass.
If they're dead, pick a random
stranger and make them do word
problems. Someone has got to pay.

8

When you get back to
your desk, notice that
you chair, your phone,
the vial you keep the true
prince's tears in are still
there. They waited for you.
This is another way
of saying no.

*

The thing about a dandelion
is when you've blown on it,
it's gone. This is another way
of pretending that you knew
all along how bad loss
would get when it finally
left you.

9

When you sneak out, open
your mouth to take in the world.
A cloud drooping low enough,
light looking for something to bounce
off, dirt, pollen, all of it will fill
your belly, but light and dust burn
off quick. This is why you shouldn't
move; energy is precious. If you speak
at the wrong time, it will leak out.
And you're saving it for a better day.

*

If none of this makes sense, it may
be time for a snack. The difference
between chocolate and mud
is time and a certain kind
of attention. Another way of saying
this is, if you're stupid enough
to love anything, you might
as well eat it.

10

When you eat, cut the box's
heart out, arrange its innards
in a star and ask it the secrets
of digestion. There is a ghost
in your cubicle. Each night,
when you leave, it throws
a little party. All the other ghosts
come and bitch about the living.
This is why your keyboard
is wonky in the mornings.
Even the dead are having
more fun than you.

*

One way to avoid intimacy
is to name yourself after a song
no one has heard. Then, when
people ask you about it, you
can explain it until they turn
away in disgust.

11

When you sleep with eyes open, know
that you won't rest. Lava burns
its own path to the sea. Remember
the time you asked lava out
on a date? It showed up on time,
was a good conversationalist,
and wanted to see you again.
You forgot where you'd parked,
and have been wandering that
parking lot ever since.

*

The one thing you wished you'd
been taught was how to burn, but school
is a series of coatings with flame
retardant. At the end, you're revealed
to a world of water. The prizes
go to those who best complain
of the damp.

12

When you leave, realize the lie:
you can always go home. Nothing
changes except ways of seeing
the stoplight. Also, bodies, places, states
of matter, and everything else.
Another way of saying this is that
everything leaves you but you'll
never pay back your student loans.

*

[woman walking, head down, in sunlight]
[car jerking toward a man in a crosswalk]
[waiting]
[pollen coats cars, tinting the view green or yellow]
[brash voice nearby]

13

When you arrive home, try
not to think about her. She
isn't thinking about you. Or,
she is. What does it matter?
A broken plan can never
be re-glued. They used
to make that stuff from dead
horses. Who wants to be a party
to that? What did horses
ever do to you? Smell like grass
and sunshine? Make you think
of running free?

*

Once you've had enough
caffeine, certain things
will become clear. The heartbeat
of the debt collectors hiding
in your closet. The faint whiff
of gasoline. The way to avoid
thinking too much is to burn
out the fuses. Everyone else
in the world is doing something
important right now while you
can't figure out why your foot
keeps going numb when you
sit on it.

14

When you wait, Death holds
his breath. There's time,
which is the biggest threat of all.
Here is how you make a process
document for loneliness: begin with
the executive overview, which
is all anyone will read. A list
of stakeholders, i.e. those responsible,
i.e. yourself. A table of contents.
Now that we've cleared out the weak-
willed, include a thousand pages
on the dietary preferences of the worms.
It's only polite to season oneself
appropriately.

*

[a TV show you won't remember
in a year is important enough
to risk your job over]

[a scheduled time to grieve]

[remember when your shirts fit?]

[it's not jealousy so much as
a wish for quiet]

15

When you sleep, flames
flicker behind your eyes.
You'll wake, to the neighbor's
fists on the wall, their complaints
about the smell of smoke.

How long has it been since
your bed caught fire? Maybe
you're not dead yet. Maybe
you have been all along.
Smile. It was all a lie. Everything
you've ever done sits waiting
for you to get it right. Every face
that ever followed you is open
and still soft. You are so tired.
You want to be done. But you
haven't even begun.